PREDICTIONS

Written by Bridget Reed
Tarot card illustrations by Colin Howard

Published by Kudos, an imprint of Top That! Publishing plc.
Copyright © 2004 Top That! Publishing plc,
Tide Mill Way, Woodbridge, Suffolk, IP12 IAP.
www.kudosbooks.com

Kudos is a Trademark of Top That! Publishing plc

All rights reserved

Contents

Introduction	4	Crystals	95
The Millennium	6	Numerology	96
The History	8	Chinese Astrology	102
Nostradamus	12	Astrology	106
Joan of Arc	16	Dreams	112
Sixth Sense	18	Reading Tea Leaves	114
Palmistry	20	Dice Prediction	118
Scrying	26	Dowsing & Divining	120
Prophecy/Psychic Ability	30	Pendulum Power	122
Tarot	34	Aura Reading	124
Rune Stones	86	Conclusion	128

Introduction

PREDICTION IS VERY DIFFICULT

"Prediction is very difficult, especially about the future."
— *Nils Bohr, Nobel Laureate in Physics*

Ever wondered who you're going to marry or which career you'll end up in? From weather reports to stock market prediction, everyone wants to know what lies ahead. In today's troubled times, people are searching for the answers to whether or not life is just random or if there is a pre-determined plan for us all.

Most of us have some fear of the future and the varied paths we will tread in years to come. Attempting to predict the future is a way to allay those fears. It helps us to avoid passively waiting for something to happen to us, and gives us a feeling of empowerment.

From ancient Chinese oracles to the divine teachings of India, there are thousands of traditions that all make claim to predicting the future. This book aims to introduce you to the most common practices.

THE MILLENNIUM

THE HERE AND NOW

For centuries, the end of the last millennium had been prophesied as being the Apocalypse – the last day of the world as we know it.

Although the world had passed through numerous thousand-year cycles before, everyone seemed to be worried about the year 2000. Maybe it was because the year ends in zeros, or because the turn of the millennium is so much grander than the roll over of a mere century.

The Millennium

THE HERE AND NOW

Common predictions were related to the return of Jesus Christ, the appearance of the Antichrist, the battle of Armageddon, atomic wars, and visitors from outer space. People feared catastrophes that would destroy much of human civilisation, cause computer program failures and general doom beyond the bounds of imagination.

Fuelling the fear of millions, were numerous books, magazine articles, talk shows, manuals and websites advising us to to get ready for the coming Apocalypse – with bunkers full of torches, gold bars, bottled water and self-defence weapons. Authorities warned of possible power failures, plane crashes and a technological shutdown as the clock struck midnight on 31 December, 1999. In preparation for the Y2K crisis, the Government of the United States alone created more committees, action weeks, budget reports, Presidential councils and orders, Congressional Acts and web pages than there were for AIDS and global warming combined – two genuine crises that actually do kill people and threaten the well-being of our planet.

THE HISTORY

A LONG AND WINDING ROAD

Centuries long ago, soothsayers and mystics often relied on nature to predict the future. In the Stone Age, fate was considered to be in the hands of the gods and nature. Primitive man attributed all natural disasters and conditions to the mood of the deities, so mystics attempted to decipher birds' cries and prophets tried to unravel the patterns of the stars to unlock the gods' secrets. Although modern methods are varied, and often complex, most have their roots in traditional, ancestral practices. Each culture has its own examples the following are just a few of them.

When Native American tribe members needed guidance, they would come before the six elders. One elder would motion to the seeker to pull a wolf's tooth and a bear's claw – all symbols of individual animals – from his medicine bag, and place them on the ground. The selection of items and their placement was interpreted by another elder, and used to read the situation, foretell the future, and give guidance to the seeker of wisdom. It is this simple ceremony that forms the basis of the modern-day medicine cards which feature different animals, each offering that creature's corresponding powers of healing and enlightenment.

THE HISTORY

A LONG AND WINDING ROAD

The ancient Celts used a wide variety of divination methods, including casting Ogham sticks (inscribed with the Druid symbolic alphabet, Ogham), interpreting dreams, illumination (where initiates stayed in a dark place, such as an underground chamber for days to undergo sensory deprivation) and consulting the tree oracle (a set of cards each representing a different tree).

The Inuit people of North America used drum divination (interpreting the beating of a drum painted with symbols; and bone divination) cracking the shoulder bone of a reindeer or caribou and interpreting the pattern made by the cracks – to seek guidance about matters such as where to hunt or where to move the settlement.

THE HISTORY

A LONG AND WINDING ROAD

In Greek and Roman times, divination was practised through the casting of lots, the flight and behaviour of birds, the behaviour of sacrificial animals and the condition of their vital organs, various omens, or sounds and dreams. They often referred to oracles, who appeared at temples. The oracles' answers to questions were supposed to express the will of the gods.

The Delphic oracle, dedicated to Apollo, was the most important in ancient Greece. A priestess spoke oracular messages whilst in a trance. These were then interpreted by a priest and given to the questioner in the form of verse and riddles. There is some evidence that drugs such as opium, henbane and hellebore were used to induce the priestess's trance.

NOSTRADAMUS

PREDICTIONS

Probably the most famous non-Biblical prophet was the Frenchman Michel de Notredame, whose predictions of the future have mystified scholars for more than 400 years. Nostradamus made over one thousand predictions, half of which, according to some historians, have already come true.

Although he died in 1566, he is said to have predicted the French Revolution and named Pasteur, Franco and Mussolini. He foretold both World Wars, the atomic bomb in Hiroshima, the Cuban Missile Crisis, the Cultural Revolution of China, and other disturbing events.

In 1555, Nostradamus published the book 'Centuries'. Each chapter was called a century, and contained 100 poems, each of four lines, called quatrains. To protect himself from the superstitious witch-hunters of the time, he wrote the quatrains in an amalgamation of French, Latin, Greek and anagrams. He even mixed up the quatrains so they weren't in chronological order.

Nostradamus often spoke of three powerful, evil dictators, whom he referred to as Antichrists. The first of these is thought to have been Napoleon Boneparte.

NOSTRADAMUS

PREDICTIONS

He describes this first Antichrist as an emperor born near Italy. Napoleon was born on the island of Corsica, near Italy:

> An Emperor will be born near Italy,
> who will cost the Empire very dearly.
> They will say, when they see his allies,
> that he is less a prince than a butcher.
>
> *Century 1 ? Quatrain 60*

Experts agree that the second Antichrist he referred to was Hitler:

> From the very depths of the west of Europe,
> a young child will be born of poor people,
> he who by his tongue will seduce a great troop:
> his fame will increase towards the realm of the east.
>
> *Century 3 ? Quatrain 35*

NOSTRADAMUS

PREDICTIONS

According to Nostradamus, the third Antichrist is more evil than the others combined. He says that this terrifying person will come from the Middle East and will lead his forces on an invasion through Europe. Some believe this to be Saddam Hussein, the Iraqi dictator. Some think it could be Osama bin Laden. Others are of the opinion that he has not yet appeared.

JOAN OF ARC

VOICES FROM GOD

"Before seven years are passed, the English will lose a greater wager than they have already done at Orléans; they will lose everything in France."

Joan of Arc

From the age of thirteen, Joan heard what she called her 'voices' or 'counsel'. She recognised these voices as angels, such as St Michael, St Margaret and St Catherine. Joan was always reluctant to speak of her voices.

In 1431, Joan of Arc predicted that within seven years, the English would be driven out of France. When asked how she knew this, she replied that it was made known to her by revelation. The English lost Paris in 1436. Her prediction had come true, but on 30th May, 1431, the English still had powerful allies in France, and Joan was burned at the stake.

SIXTH SENSE

DO WE HAVE ONE?

Everyone is aware of the five basic senses: seeing, touching, smelling, hearing and tasting. Some psychologists, however, believe that everyone has a sixth sense – a connection to something greater than their physical senses are able to perceive. It is this that allows us to delve into the future.

Carl Jung, one of the founders of modern psychoanalysis, maintained that the true value of predicting the future with divinatory tools, such as runes, had nothing to do with prophecy, but was our way of exploring the subconscious.

Spiritualists believe that every human being is equipped from birth with this sixth sense, and that all that is required to access it is 'tuning in' to another person's frequency or to the frequency of someone in the spirit world. Electronic tuning is done through means that are mechanical in nature. Spiritual tuning is done through the brain with mental focus, intent and desire being the means of achieving this.

PALMISTRY

THE STUDY OF THE HAND

Palmistry, the science based on studying the lines and mounts on our hands and investigating their significance, was first practised thousands of years ago in the East. It most probably originated in India and has been passed down through the generations by word of mouth.

Today, as well as for divination, hand analysis is now used in scientific, genetic, psychological and forensic fields, for the purposes of recruitment, character and personality assessment, medical research, criminal identification and crime detection.

Palmistry is referred to in manuscripts from India and China, dated as early as 3200 BC. Information on the laws and practice of hand reading has been found in Vedic scripts, the Bible and early Semitic writings. Notable people such as Aristotle, Hippocrates, Paracelsus, Fludd and Julius Caesar, were all practised palmists. However, the practice of palmistry was forced underground by the Catholic Church during the sixteenth century, who associated it with the devil. It re-emerged in the mid-seventeenth century in England, and continued to grow and develop throughout the 20th century, and into the 21st.

Modern palmistry is made up of four main elements: chirognomy (the study of the shape of fingers, thumbs and palms to suggest character and personality); dermatoglyphics (the study of the skin patterns of hands); gesture (the study of hand and body movement); and chiromancy (the study of lines and features of a palm) which is briefly covered in the following pages.

PALMISTRY

HEAD LINE

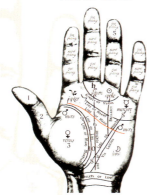

The most important line of all, representing the way we think, reason, and view the world.

If the line is less marked on the left hand, you are more likely to have a positive personality and vice versa.

A longer line indicates imagination, more flexibility and openness to suggestions. The more deeply etched the line, the more egotistical the owner.

LIFE LINE

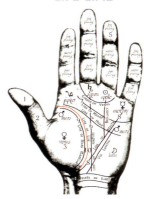

The Life line reveals quality of life and physical well-being. It is also a measure of energy, vitality and endurance.

If it is a single line, you are self-reliant. When the line is open-ended (you may need a magnifying glass to see), this suggests a heavily dependent nature.

If the line on the right hand sweeps out into the palm, you are independent. The reverse suggests someone who is stuck in a rut.

PALMISTRY

HEART LINE

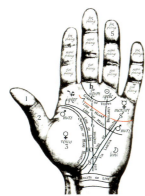

This is associated with our emotions and how they affect our personalities.

The more deeply etched the line, the more emotional or health problems there are. A faint line suggests a person who may be cold, and unemotional in nature.

A Heart line set low in the palm implies an extremely passionate nature, but high in the palm indicates a person's hardness.

FATE LINE

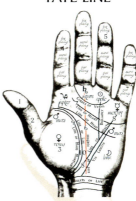

This line shows our path through life. It is also known as the line of awareness, career, destiny, fortune and duty.

If the line appears on the left hand only, this suggests lots of dreams but no action. If it appears on the right hand only, the subject is appreciative of life but unwilling to bother changing it.

When formed on both hands, the owner is well-balanced and attuned to life. If it is absent, they have no ambition and are inwardly unsettled.

PALMISTRY

SUN LINE

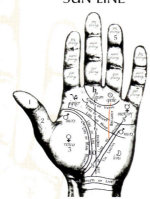

The Sun, or Apollo line, is a sister to the Fate line. It can be mistaken for the Mercury or Health line.

If found in some form, the owner is talented and prepared to work hard. If it begins inside the Life line, the owner will find their family helpful throughout their life.

The further up the palm it starts, the greater the owner's persistence in achieving their ambitions. With a forked start, they may have more than one string to their bow.

MERCURY LINE

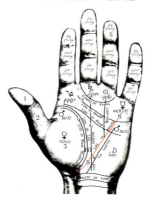

This is also known as the Health line, or Hepatica line.

If this line is found, there will be a physical weakness, possibly lasting or recurring. The owner may also be obsessed with diet and fitness.

When it starts inside the Life line, the person is a natural worrier, in extreme cases and hypochondriacal occasionally.

PALMISTRY

SIMIAN LINE

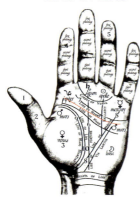

This is, strictly speaking, a fusion of the Head line with the Heart line. It frequently appears on the hands of obsessive people who feel driven to succeed.

People with a Simian line are intelligent leaders who will remain hard in order to get the job done, disposing of any niceties.

A thick line straight across the palm indicates a selfish and materialistic nature. If found on the right hand only, the owner is likely to have a Jekyll and Hyde personality.

RASCETTES LINES

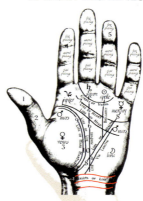

The Rascettes, or Bracelets, are the lines that run across the inside of the wrist at the base of the palm.

Three well-formed lines are known as the 'magic bracelet', and this symbolises good luck and immunity to travel sickness.

Any arches in the bracelets can signify problems or weaknesses in the body – from the bladder to reproductive ailments.

SCRYING

THE ART OF LOOKING

Derived from the English word 'descry' which means 'to make out dimly' or 'to reveal', scrying is the ancient act of divination for the purpose of clairvoyance.

It is usually achieved by concentrating on, or staring at, an object with a reflective surface until dream-like visions appear. This object is normally a crystal ball, however some people can achieve visions from gazing into flames or even a shallow bowl of water or black ink.

Used in ancient times, scrying is one of the oldest methods of divination. It was practised widely by the ancient Egyptians and Babylonians, and developed in the Americas, Australasia and Europe.

The stereotypical image of someone scrying would be a Gypsy fortune-teller looking into her crystal ball, but magicians and witches have practised scrying for centuries. In the Middle Ages, a wise woman (or a wise man), perhaps also called a witch, with a natural gift of second sight was called upon for scrying purposes.

Although the object used for scrying usually has a shiny surface, any number of objects can be used. The Egyptians used ink, blood and other dark liquids. The Romans preferred shiny objects and stones. When attempting scrying yourself, you don't need to use a crystal ball, try water in a dark bowl or small pool, mirrors, crystals, embers in a fire at night, or the eyes of another person who is sitting opposite you in a dimly lit room.

SCRYING

THE ART OF LOOKING

Gaze steadily into the scrying surface (you can blink and allow your point of focus to wander a bit – this isn't self-torture). Eventually, you should be able to pick out shapes or images in the scrying surface. These can appear as crude sketches but sometimes they will have the clarity of a photograph.

When these images begin to form in your mind, allow your attention to focus on them. Discard the scrying surface now – it is of no more use. As the images become clearer, you will find that you know things about what you are seeing – background information will come to the front of your mind. Pay attention to what you know about the images you are seeing. Frequently, visions are symbolic and you may need to consult a trained scryer who is skilled at interpreting their meaning.

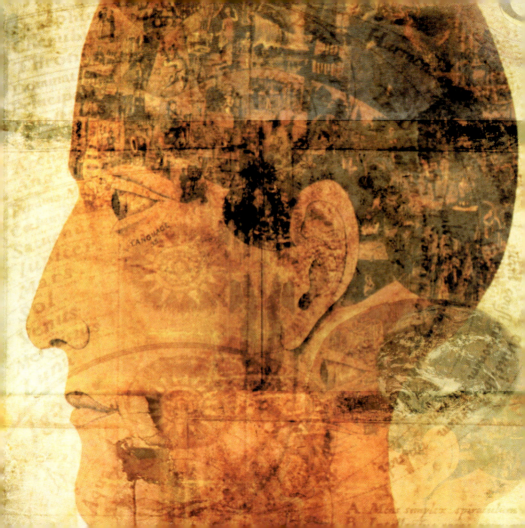

PROPHECY/PSYCHIC ABILITY

PREDICTING THE FUTURE

Since ancient times, people have believed that it is possible to predict the future.

The Temple of Apollo in Delphi, for example, housed the most important oracle of ancient Greece, known as Pythia. Only the wealthy could afford the fees of the oracle and many questions of state were decided by what the Delphic oracle foretold.

In both the Old and New Testaments of the Bible, we read of people whose dreams foretold the future and would influence the decisions of kings or pharaohs.

Chinese emperors would base their decrees upon the auguries read in the I-Ching oracle of change.

PROPHECY/PSYCHIC ABILITY

PREDICTING THE FUTURE

There has, however, been some scepticism about modern prophets. Critics claim that these so-called 'psychics' simply take current events, review the recent past, mix in a knowledge of history and then come to some fairly accurate conclusions about one thing or another. Lots of people predicted World War Two years before it happened.

Despite understandable scepticism, there are a number of prophecies and predictions that have stood the test of time. They dealt with things that hadn't even been invented when the prophet authors made their pronouncements. Neither the intellect nor the analytical mind could have influenced them, because these events came to pass many years, even centuries, later. Things like submarines, aircraft and ballistic missiles were seen in prophecies hundreds of years before they were constructed.

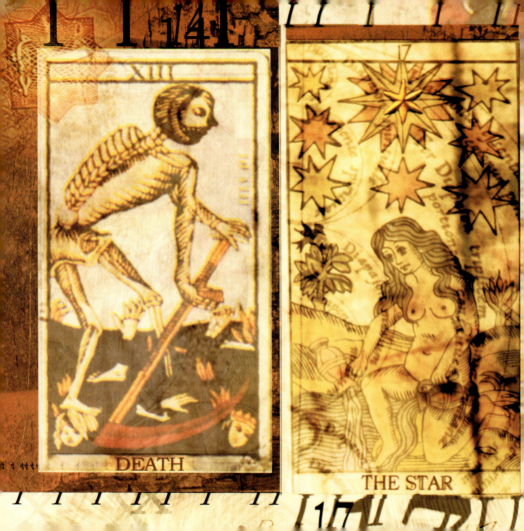

Tarot

ORIGINS

The origins of the tarot are unknown; it has been linked with the Italian Renaissance, ancient Egypt, the Middle East and Western Gypsies. However, it is commonly regarded as the most highly evolved method of divination in European civilisation.

Tarot cards are comprised of two types, the Major Arcana, consisting of 22 cards, and the Minor Arcana, which consists of 56 cards. Each card is a symbolic picture, and when the cards are set out in a 'spread', they can be read and interpreted.

The cards are used to gain insight into situations, and to predict the future. Working with the tarot is not only a method of divination, but also a way of completely accepting yourself and becoming inwardly enlightened.

Tarot

MAJOR ARCANA

 From the very beginning, the Major Arcana of the Tarot have fascinated people with their complexity. The 22 cards, called 'trumps', correspond to things that lie very deep in our psyche, our intuition.

Tarot

MAJOR ARCANA

The cards form a sequence of 21 numbered cards, plus one numberless card called the Fool, which is sometimes numbered zero. There is a specific order to the Major Arcana cards, but some decks deviate from this.

The cards of Justice and Strength are most commonly transposed, for example this occurs in the popular Rider-Waite Tarot deck. Each of the Major Arcana cards depicts a strange scene which appears to tell a story or convey a message. You should be careful when reading, as every card of the Major Arcana has creative and destructive opposing sides.

If a card is laid with the image upside down from the view point of the person reading the card, it is considered 'reversed'. In both the Major and Minor Arcana, this will usually indicate the negative, the opposite of the upright card. Since the Major Arcana are more significant in a spread, it is only those cards that have their reverse meanings expanded upon in this book.

TAROT

THE FOOL

Upright
This card represents individuality, new experiences and new beginnings requiring wisdom and courage. It also symbolises being carefree, impulsive and enthusiastic.

Reversed
The reverse of this card is recklessness, childishness and a lack of motivation.

THE MAGICIAN

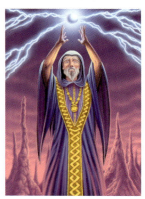

Upright
Also known as the Cobbler, this is a very creative card. It represents imagination, willpower, confidence, creative energy, communication and skill.

Reversed
The reverse means indecision, a weak will or the misuse of skills or powers.

Tarot

THE HIGH PRIESTESS

Upright
The High Priestess is a complicated card, representing a woman's sexuality and yet virginity at the same time. It also symbolises wise judgment, animation and strong creative abilities.

Reversed
The reverse means poor judgement and conceit.

THE EMPRESS

Upright
This card symbolises fertility, domestic life, fruitfulness, inspiration and positive achievement. It is also the symbol of beauty and grace.

Reversed
The reverse is extravagance, greed, laziness and wastefulness.

TAROT

THE EMPEROR

Upright
Represents worldly wealth and power, strength and confidence. It focuses on energy, organisation, vision and ability.

Reversed
The reverse means weakness, immaturity and an obsession with fame and fortune.

THE HIERPHANT

Upright
Also known as the High Priest, this is the spiritual father of the deck. He is a teacher, a mentor, a leader – especially of traditional values. This card represents kindness and a desire to conform.

Reversed
The reverse is delayed ambitions and kindness to the point of foolishness.

TAROT

THE LOVERS

Upright
This card symbolises a loving relationship, friendship and harmony. It also means choice, decisions, and a balance of male and female energies.

Reversed
The reverse is frustrated romance or infidelity.

THE CHARIOT

Upright
Symbolises struggle and triumph against the odds, prestige, self-control, drive, willpower, focus and bravado. It implies mastery, conquest and triumph.

Reversed
The reverse of this means failure, collapse of plans and vanity.

TAROT

JUSTICE

Upright
Represents balanced objectivity and outlook, sincerity, harmony and equilibrium.

Reversed
The reverse side represents injustice, indecision and difficult adjustments.

HERMIT

Upright
This card symbolises a teacher and guide. It represents enlightenment and the need to choose an unfamiliar path.

Reversed
The reverse of this is mistaken advice and excessive caution.

TAROT

THE WHEEL OF FORTUNE

Upright
Represents unexpected events, wisdom gained from experience, changes, a new cycle, a turn of the wheel, a progression or a movement.

Reversed
The reverse means failed enterprise or a difficult change.

STRENGTH

Upright
This card represents spiritual or physical strength and triumph.

Reversed
The reverse is weakness, sickness, lack of faith or the abuse of power.

TAROT

THE HANGED MAN

Upright
Symbolises willing sacrifice, lack of progress, stamina and changing directions or perspectives.

Reversed
The reverse indicates futile sacrifice and selfishness.

DEATH

Upright
This card means unwelcome change leading to a rebirth, changes, renewal, and destruction (but not sudden or radical destruction).

Reversed
The reverse represents stagnation and fear of change.

Tarot

TEMPERANCE

Upright
Means moderation, compromise, harmony and mixing separate elements into a whole.

Reversed
The reverse is conflict, lack of harmony, hostility, frustration and impatience.

THE DEVIL

Upright
Symbolises self-indulgence, greed, controversy and a self-preservation instinct. It can also mean temptation, lust, narrowness, animal nature, danger, ambition and obsession.

Reversed
The reverse means liberation and healing.

TAROT

THE TOWER

Upright
Represents unexpected events and a temporary loss of stability. It can also mean catastrophic and irreversible change, on almost every conceivable level.

Reversed
The reverse symbolises destroyed ambition and boredom.

THE STAR

Upright
Means hope, love, rebirth, pleasure, satisfaction, purpose and guidance.

Reversed
The reverse represents disappointment, pessimism, crushed dreams, bad luck and imbalance.

TAROT

THE MOON

Upright
This is the card of the subconscious, and refers to those things which are hidden and sometimes feared. It represents imagination, uncertainty and fluctuation.

Reversed
The reverse means minor deceptions avoided.

THE SUN

Upright
This card represents satisfaction, gratitude, health, happiness, strength, inspiration and liberation.

Reversed
The reverse is a lack of confidence and mild unhappiness.

TAROT

JUDGEMENT

Upright
This card is also known as Rejuvenation. It symbolises development, resolution and release.

Reversed
The reverse is transient success, loss and delay.

THE WORLD

Upright
Represents completion, reward, celebration and success. It is closely related to the meaning and symbolisation of the circle.

Reversed
The reverse is disappointment, lack of vision and inconclusion.

TAROT

MINOR ARCANA – CUPS

The word 'arcana' means 'mysteries' or 'secrets'.

The 56 cards of the Minor Arcana are divided into four suits, each suit having ten cards (1–10) and four court cards (Page, Knight, Queen and King).

The suit of cups symbolises romance, friendship, creativity and sociability.

The reverse of this suit means jealousy, pain, rejection, excessive love of luxury and pre-occupation with one's self.

TAROT

ACE OF CUPS

This card means the beginning of great love, and may indicate a pregnancy.

It suggests inner attunement and spirituality. Cups are the suit of the heart, and the Ace stands for the instinctive knowledge that comes from within. Trust what your feelings are telling you.

TWO OF CUPS

This card often means an engagement or marriage.

Whenever two forces are drawn together, there is the potential for bonding. The Two of Cups card can stand for the union of any two entities – people, groups, ideas or talents.

tarot

THREE OF CUPS

In readings, the Three of Cups can signify friendship.

This card can represent community – the network of support created when we interact with others. It can be any group in which the members feel a bond. The Three of Cups card stands for all forms of support, including formal aid such as counselling and other social services.

FOUR OF CUPS

This card can represent a positive period of self-reflection and renewal.

By taking the time to go within to dream, muse and reflect, you restore your emotional balance. The Four of Cups also represents kindness from other people.

TAROT

FIVE OF CUPS

This card represents loss, regret or denial in varying degrees.

It could be tangible (the break-up of a relationship), or intangible (loss of opportunity). This card can also warn you of forthcoming loss and help to reduce its toll.

SIX OF CUPS

This card represents happy feelings coming from the past and innocence – a word with many shades of meaning.

You can be innocent in the strictly legal sense of lack of guilt. There are lots of possibilities that can apply to the Six of Cups, depending on the situation.

TAROT

SEVEN OF CUPS

This is a card of illusions and deceptions.

Making a hasty decision, therefore, could be as bad as being unable to make any decision. When the Seven of Cups appears in a reading, think carefully about all your options.

EIGHT OF CUPS

This can be a card of separation or divorce.

It can imply a literal move or trip, especially from an established home to a new, unknown one in an unknown land. The Eight of Cups stands for those moments when we realise that the past is truly gone.

TAROT

NINE OF CUPS

This is sometimes called the 'wish' card.

What you have an appetite for, you will be given, and your wish will come true. On an emotional level, it indicates that relationships are loving and complete. Creativity is at a high, friendships and emotions are good.

TEN OF CUPS

This is a card of joy, love and friendship.

It represents the kind of family we all work to create, a family we can trust and rely on. The questioner can be told that this family – or family of friends – can be, or is, theirs.

TAROT

PAGE OF CUPS

This card stands for romance, deep feelings and the inner life.

In readings, the Page of Cups suggests that an opening may appear that stirs your emotions, pulls at your heart strings or brings you great joy. When you see such a chance, act on it! The page is rooted in a world of inner images, fantasy and creative ideas.

KNIGHT OF CUPS

The Knight of Cups represents balanced objectivity and outlook, sincerity, harmony and equilibrium.

If your life needs balance, it may be time for a change.

TAROT

QUEEN OF CUPS

In readings, the Queen of Cups is someone in touch with her emotions, who asks you to think about your own feelings.

The Queen can represent someone who is like her, or an atmosphere of love, acceptance and respect for feelings.

KING OF CUPS

The King of Cups asks you to take the kind of action he might take.

For example, responding calmly in a crisis, using diplomacy rather than force, reaching out to help, or accepting a different point of view. This card can also represent an atmosphere of caring and tolerance.

TAROT

MINOR ARCANA – WANDS

The Suit of Wands stands for creative integrity, security, positive relationships and inner development.

The reverse is disrupted work, laziness, ignorance and romantic jealousy.

TAROT

ACE OF WANDS

When this card appears in a reading it often signifies the beginning of new life.

It could indicate a pregnancy, or mean the beginning of a whole new phase in life. In order to confirm pregnancy, you need to look for other 'baby' cards like the Page of Cups, or the Ace or Three of Cups.

TWO OF WANDS

The card indicates that we are in charge of the way that our life is unfolding.

The Two of Wands does not rule out the occasional pleasant surprise, or obstacle, but it does allow us to fulfil our needs and chase our destiny.

TAROT

THREE OF WANDS

This card – The Lord of Virtue – represents our trueness to our own inner needs and inspirations.

It represents a point of inner balance where we are clear about the things we want to create in our life. Out of this clarity and confidence arises a new quality of self-reliance and happiness.

FOUR OF WANDS

The Lord of Completion marks a point where a circle has been completed.

It can apply to work projects, personal situations and even phases of our life. In some respects it's like a lesser reflection of the World, the final Major Arcana card.

TAROT

FIVE OF WANDS

The Lord of Strife usually appears in a reading to indicate quarrels, conflict and discord.

There is rarely anything of value to be gained from the disharmony introduced by this card – in fact, it will often indicate argument for arguments sake.

SIX OF WANDS

The Lord of Victory is a card of fight, competition and eventual victory.

It applies to areas of our life where we feel we have had to fight very hard to achieve our goals, and at points when we have had to contest our position strongly.

SEVEN OF WANDS

The Seven of Wands indicates that you are facing one of those momentous happenings in your life.

It advises you to believe in yourself and go forward. It is a card about encountering demanding situations, and having the courage to be true to your own desires, ambitions and needs.

EIGHT OF WANDS

This card will often represent the type of cathartic discussion which ends confusion.

The Eight of Wands always brings a new surge of energy and freshness when it appears. It often signals entry into a new phase or project – one which stands a good chance of success.

TAROT

NINE OF WANDS

Lord of Strength, reminds us that being true to ourselves will release energies to help us to deal with whatever we find within.

When it appears, we can be reassured that our inner strength will guide us toward our goals.

TEN OF WANDS

If a situation marked by the Ten of Wands becomes prolonged, we will begin to feel trapped and deeply unhappy.

If you ever read on a specific situation, and this card comes up in the final position, the reading is probably telling you not to waste any more effort on a conflict that you cannot win. Sometimes we are better off just walking away.

TAROT

PAGE OF WANDS

The person symbolised by the Page of Wands is a young man who seizes every opportunity with childlike innocence.

He is inspired by, but does not challenge, the exchange of intense viewpoints. In love, he symbolises intense faithfulness.

KNIGHT OF WANDS

The Knight of Wands signifies a departure from challenge.

He is unsure of commitment and cannot confront his own feelings. In positive terms, this card indicates that one may have escaped difficulties.

TAROT

QUEEN OF WANDS

This card represents a passionate female who wants to rouse people into action through her outspoken and critical nature.

Although she appears to be fighting those that cross her, she is a true champion of anyone she supports.

KING OF WANDS

This King supports our creative efforts, and motivates our ambitions upholding the principles of integrity.

Beware of relying on him though, as he cannot devote all his efforts to one cause. He has the same intense capacity for romantic passion that he applies to his creative work and can push us to persevere in seeking the highest of unions.

TAROT

MINOR ARCANA – PENTACLES

The suit of Pentacles symbolises generosity, financial reward, success at work and craftsmanship.

The reverse of the suit is meanness, covetousness, poverty, unemployment and isolation.

TAROT

ACE OF PENTACLES

The Ace of Pentacles marks, on the everyday level, the start of a new project, which is likely to be successful.

So it will come up to show a new job, or a new business venture. Usually this will be the sort of project that seems to continually grow, with each level of attainment producing – almost of itself – the next step of the journey.

TWO OF PENTACLES

The Lord of Change, this card indicates the necessity of constant change in our life if we are not to stagnate.

It often marks a turning point – a new job, a shift of fortune or a change of home. When this card appears, it demands a thorough re-assessment of our overall position and willingness to go with the chances that come our way.

TAROT

THREE OF PENTACLES

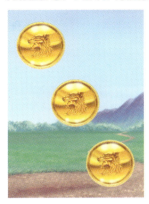

This is a card that teaches attainment through effort and marks achievement in the working area.

It advises us to keep the pressure on so you maintain momentum, and to pay attention to detail. It sometimes marks a period where all energies will be channelled into one project, to the exclusion of everything else.

FOUR OF PENTACLES

The Lord of Power represents the time when we achieve a stable level of material balance – at least at that moment in time.

On a purely mundane level, it might appear after settling into a new home. The card is, at this level, much concerned with material bounty.

TAROT

FIVE OF PENTACLES

This card indicates worries, such as an unexpected expense, job concerns or maybe even a disturbance in family life.

But whatever is causing the problem is much more of a threat than a reality. Worrying about it might just make it worse than it needs to be!

SIX OF PENTACLES

The Lord of Success is a card full of the promise of bounty.

When we have achieved a degree of inner confidence and self-belief, we release new streams of energy which create a powerful and rewarding reality around ourselves. New ideas are easy to implement, and new projects are fruitful. We are energised and enthusiastic about the work we have in hand.

TAROT

SEVEN OF PENTACLES

This card represents a fear of failure. Be patient, and don't rush.

Self-control will win the day. If you have a run of bad financial fortune, it's time to examine your reactions. If you believe you'll fail, then you surely will. We have a major role in creating our own reality. If we expect negative things, we are inviting them into our lives.

EIGHT OF PENTACLES

This card predicts the need to progress with caution.

It is a card of starting over, of doing something new, or a period of expansion. Apprenticeship can be scary or demoralising, and it foretells, if not a tough period, a time of learning and mistakes, doubts and just hard work.

TAROT

NINE OF PENTACLES

This card means profit or gain.

It signifies a lucky windfall or payment for work well done – enough to buy what you most desire.

TEN OF PENTACLES

This card represents abundance, wealth, and gain.

It is the pinnacle of prosperity, with material goods that last instead of being temporary; this is a family home bought and paid for, a business that you can pass on to your children. You might find yourself the lucky recipient of a trust fund or a lottery win big enough to last a lifetime.

TAROT

PAGE OF PENTACLES

The Page symbolises fresh opportunities, usually in the form of a task, activity or job involving some responsibility.

He advocates tackling challenges with confidence, and not worrying about the consequences. By adhering to this strategy, there will be a positive outcome.

KNIGHT OF PENTACLES

This is the firmest, and least impetuous of the Knights.

Do not underestimate him, however, or take his calm exterior for granted. When a job has to be done quickly and comprehensively, give it to the Knight of Pentacles. as he is the most trustworthy of all of the Knights.

TAROT

QUEEN OF PENTACLES

The Queen of Pentacles is a nurturer a practical, and down-to-earth one.

Always there to help, in a material or tangible way. She encourages and promotes positive utilisation of creativity. She also has a serious and introverted side however.

KING OF PENTACLES

Known for his generosity, the King of Pentacles has worked hard for his money and is successful.

He expects those whom he has helped to help themselves. He is very grounded and lives in harmony with the land over which he rules. Despite his strength, power and riches, he is not an overly proud or arrogant man. He has a true estimate of his worth.

TAROT

MINOR ARCANA - SWORDS

The suit of Swords means strength, courage, hope and peace amid strife, and a successful journey.

The reverse means spiritual suffering, loneliness, sacrifice, loss and defeat.

TAROT

ACE OF SWORDS

The Ace of Swords stands for the ability to see things from a clear perspective.

When this card rules, we are able to remove the confusion which tends to cloud our judgment. We can see what is important and worth fighting for. It can also enable us to identify the 'red herrings' that prevent us thinking clearly.

TWO OF SWORDS

The Two of Swords indicates that a painful and difficult situation is being reconciled.

However, in this context, it is very important to look carefully at the cards which follow it, as there is a possibility that a relationship will never be exactly the same as it was before the conflict or quarrel.

TAROT

THREE OF SWORDS

The Lord of Sorrow almost always indicates some sort of disruption which will cause pain and uncertainty.

Such disruption leads to a loss of balance and disharmony in daily life.

FOUR OF SWORDS

The Lord of Truce marks a period where we are able to rest and recover, after a difficult time in our life.

It will appear after trauma, the breakdown of a relationship; a troublesome and worrying time financially; or an operation or a major illness.

FIVE OF SWORDS

This card generally appears to indicate that we are in for some disappointment or loss.

The reversed Five of Swords represents a lesser chance of defeat or an empty victory.

SIX OF SWORDS

The Lord of Science appears in a reading when we have passed through a stormy or difficult time.

We have come through this time and into the safety of a sheltered harbour, where we can recuperate, and consider the difficulties which have arisen around us.

TAROT

SEVEN OF SWORDS

The Lord of Futility represents the times in life where we feel too overwhelmed and doubtful to act decisively towards our problems.

It will usually appear when there are difficult decisions to be made, or when situations arise that require we take action. When we are weary, feeling over-stressed and helpless, we do nothing. As a result, of course, things inevitably get worse.

EIGHT OF SWORDS

The Lord of Interference is the card that comes up to indicate deliberate or accidental interference with the natural flow of energy.

It often signals problems with endurance, inability to make decisions, lack of concentration on important details, and overall disturbance.

TAROT

NINE OF SWORDS

The Lord of Cruelty is never a happy card to emerge in a reading.

It always indicates hardness and unkindness, a total lack of consideration or compassion. This cruelty appears in a way that suggests a harsh naturalness to the process of inflicting pain.

TEN OF SWORDS

The Ten of Swords stands for the power in our mind which allows us to fulfil our dreams, beliefs and aspirations.

If we have believed in our worthiness to achieve and attain, we will inevitably have attracted joy, happiness and success into our life.

TAROT

PAGE OF SWORDS

The Page of Swords can indicate receiving a message which contains important information.

He may be testing your reaction to dramas created for this purpose and warns against rash decisions. Another aspect of this Page is the subconscious, which contains the genius leading to moments of great clarity and intuition.

KNIGHT OF SWORDS

The Knight of Swords symbolises the insecure mind that refuses to take another's feelings or opinions into account.

If anyone gets in the way of his swinging sword, he will strike them down. But the card can also symbolise being very goal-orientated.

TAROT

QUEEN OF SWORDS

The Queen of Swords has a cold and emotionally detached way of dealing with the world.

In a reading, the Queen speaks of standing up to people, making demands and being clear about one's needs.

KING OF SWORDS

Similar to the King of Cups, the King of Swords carries an aura of intimidation. Both are silent and serious.

By tradition, the King of Swords is an expert on law, politics, society or communication. Wherever he is found, he exercises power. He is emotionally cold, as is the Queen. The King of Swords is happiest with a life of stimulating work following high ideals.

TAROT

BASIC READINGS

There are many methods of laying out the cards when reading. It makes little difference which method you choose; just use the one which appeals to you most.

PAST EVENTS

PRESENT

FUTURE EVENTS

Before you do a reading, begin by shuffling the cards. Generally it is best to draw the cards 'blind' (set them out face down) so that you can respond objectively to the pictures.

A simple reading is to draw three cards from the pack, representing the past, present and future. Another way is to select one card a day, to meditate upon. This helps you to become more aware of yourself and your needs.

TAROT

THE FAIR CARD

The more cards of the Major Arcana that appear in this spread, the more you should pay attention to that particular theme.

1. THE ANSWER/ THE FOCUS

4. FUTURE EFFECTS

2. HOW TO HANDLE THE SITUATION

3. POSSIBLE PROBLEM

It's also significant if the spread starts with the same card, such as starting and ending with a King, this is also the case if all the cards in a four-card spread are of the same suit. The odds of this happening however, are about 1 in 1,400.

TAROT

THE CELTIC CROSS SPREAD

Lay ten cards out in the position and order as shown.
Each position has its own significance, and the card that falls on it must be interpreted in the light of that position.

TAROT

The Star Spread

OUTCOME

KNOWN DESIRES

HEART OF THE QUESTION

WHAT IS YET TO UNFOLD

INTELLECT

EMOTIONS

PRESENT

Lay one card in each of the positions with a particular question in mind.

TAROT

ASTROLOGICAL SPREAD

Lay twelve cards in an imaginary circle, anti-clockwise, then deal the rest of the pack out.

10. Our Inner Self
11. Friendships
9. Travel & Wider Vision
12. Isolation & Detachment
8. Taking Risks
1. Attitude Towards Life
7. Our Partners
2. Attitude Towards Wealth
6. Thinking & Understanding
3. Practical Thinking
5. Pleasure & Entertainment
4. Emotional Comfort

Each pile represents the twelve houses of the horoscope. The cards dealt into a house indicate what is happening in the areas of your life marked on the diagram.

RUNE STONES

A GIFT FROM THE GODS

Rune stones are an ancient form of Scandinavian divination. There was a huge interest in Rune stones in the twentieth century, and they are now, in the 21st century, one of the most popular tools of divination in the Western World.

There have been many different runic alphabets in use throughout Northern Europe over the centuries. The most common is the Germanic or Elder Futhark ('futhark' is a term derived from the first six letters). This system may have begun as early as 200 BC. The word 'rune' comes from 'runa', the ancient Germanic term for a mystery or secret.

Runes became very popular throughout England and Scandinavia. In Norse mythology, the runes were claimed to be a gift to mankind from Odin, the king of the Norse gods. The Norse people consulted the runes for prediction regularly, and especially on important occasions.

RUNE STONES

A GIFT FROM THE GODS

Most modern rune sets consist of twenty five stones, one for each of the twenty four letters of the runic alphabet and a single blank stone.

Runes can be cast in any layout, or spread. Aspects are determined in essentially two ways, either by the position a rune stone falls in a casting (for example face up or face down, inside or outside a certain field), and by the angle at which one rune stone is juxtaposed to another.

The individual presents the problem. The runes are then laid out in a pattern, or thrown on a cloth or the ground, and the symbols are interpreted in relation to the problem.

The simplest reading involves drawing a single rune which will provide an overall interpretation of the situation, offering a straightforward prediction. Alternatively, drawing three rune stones allows a situation to be interpreted in depth, thus allowing for complexities. The first stone represents factors that have led up to the current situation, the second interprets it and the third offers possible outcomes.

RUNE STONES

Ansuz – the messenger rune, the god Loki.

The knowledge from this rune is regarded as a true blessing, if drawn, your call is to a new life. New connections are important so be aware of the prediction prior to meetings, visits and chance encounters, especially with those wiser than yourself.

Gebo – the rune of partnerships and giving.

Giving and receiving are regarded as an exchange of forces and an integral element of true relationships. Drawing this rune indicates that a relationship of some sort is to be expected.

Othila – separation, retreat and inheritance.

The appearance of this stone signals a time of separating paths and the severance of old selves and relationships. The Othila stone shows that one should become both submissive and retreat. It demands that you identify and abandon some part of yourself, such as a behavioural trait. Though this rune's demand is daunting your true self will as a result be revealed.

Uruz – strength, manhood, womanhood, the wild ox.

The Uruz rune marks new beginnings or a dramatic change, both instances will require great personal strength and perseverance. Primal or instinctual traits will serve you well in this time of action.

Rune Stones

Mannaz – the self.

The message of the mannaz stone is to remain modest in order to find true direction. It represents all the potentials and frailties of humanity and it is therefore important that you reflect upon your inner self and seek stillness before change.

Algiz – protection, sedge or rushes, the elk.

This stone signals that control of emotions is important, especially during times of change and development. New opportunities will arise when this stone appears. Those who draw the Aligiz rune are urged to remain mindful of the protection it offers through correct conduct, denial will prevent progress.

Eihwaz – defence, avertive powers, symbolised by the yew tree.

If there is an obstacle in your path be aware that it may prove beneficial, problems should be regarded as warnings. The Eithwaz rune offers patience and often announces a time of waiting. Instead of pressing forwards, wait for the fruit to ripen.

Inguz – represents fertility, new beginnings and Ing, the Hero God.

The drawing of this rune may foretell a time of joyful deliverance and a new path. Completion is crucial, so finish your current tasks and free yourself from a bad habit or relationship before moving on to new things.

RUNE STONES

Nauthiz – constraint, necessity and pain.

This rune represents the obstacles that we encounter and warns of delay. Be aware that you may be forced to reconsider your plans. Perseverance or a period of restoration is required in order to move on and achieve new things.

Perth – initiation, mystery, a secret matter.

This mystery rune's ways are hidden and secret. It encourages the one that draws it to let go of everything and listen to their inner self. The rune foretells of unexpected surprises and rewards.

Teiwaz – the warrior Tiw, the Sky God.

The battle of the spiritual warrior is within one's self. Patience is this rune's virtue, and with it comes knowledge. Teiwaz urges you to be brave and follow your heart. When this stone is drawn in the context of a romantic relationship, it confirms that the relationship is both timely and providential.

Kano – opening, fire, torch.

The drawing of this rune indicates it is time for you to dispel the darkness that has previously been shrouding part of your life. Kano encourages serious, clear concentration in order to allow new ideas to flow.

Rune Stones

Jera – harvest, fertile season, one year.

This rune applies to any commitment that you might have. Jera offers the comfort of success, but also advises patience. Be open to new ideas and do not be afraid.

Wunjo – joy and light.

This rune symbolises fruitfulness and the end of a journey. It expresses a time of blessing and joy. Now is the time to make plans and fulfil your ambitions, however, remember to share your joy and be aware of others.

Fehu – possession, nourishment and cattle.

The Fehu rune promises nourishment and fulfilment It encourages one to be vigilant and protect what has been gained. While you enjoy good fortune be careful to share it, as a willingness to do so is a true test of oneself.

Raido – journey, communication, union and reunion.

The appearance of this stone signals that you are not to rely entirely upon your own strength. The journey ahead of you is one of self healing and change. Be aware of any excess in your life and listen to the teacher within yourself.

Rune Stones

Hagalaz – disruption, elemental power, hail.

This stone foretells of destruction and disruption. It is often described as the Great Awakener. This event may take many forms, from an awakening of your senses to a disruption of events beyond your control. Inner strength will prevail and guide you so failure is unlikely.

Laguz – flow, water, that which conducts.

Laguz urges you to savour each moment and enjoy the experience of living. It may signal a time to cleanse and reorganise in order to strengthen the inner self.

Ehwaz – movement, progress and the horse.

This is the rune of movement and encourages the one who draws it to make the best of a situation. It suggests gradual development and growth. Whoever draws Ehwaz is ready to face the future and should share their good fortune.

Berkana – growth and rebirth, symbolised by the birch tree.

The growth that this rune suggests may concern issues of the world or the family, and will require careful consideration. The virtues of modesty, patience, fairness and generosity are also called for when this rune is drawn. With the correct attitude, the one who draws it will blossom and grow.

Rune Stones

Odin – the unknowable, the Divine.

The drawing of this rune shows that the answer you seek lies within yourself. Odin brings to the surface our deepest fears, as well as our greatest dreams.

Sowelu – wholeness, life force, the Sun's energy.

Sowelu symbolises wholeness and indicates the path we should follow. The drawing of this rune marks a time of regeneration. Reveal parts of your life that you have kept secret and hidden and let light into shadowed areas.

Isa – standstill, withdrawal, ice.

The message of this rune is to be patient during times of redundancy. It suggests that by releasing, cleansing and shedding the old you will be prepared to welcome the new. A personal sacrifice may be required when this is drawn.

Dagaz – breakthrough, transformation, day.

This rune predicts a major shift or change. Your warrior nature will reveal itself when this stone is drawn. A period of achievement is ahead of you, but hard work will be essential. Look within yourself for guidance and enlightenment.

Thurisaz – gateway, place of non-action, the god Thor.

Thurisaz indicates that your inner and outer self require improvement. The symbolism of the gateway is significant with the past behind you and the future in front. Review and accept both the victories and sorrows of your past, once you have released the past you may reclaim your inner power and step through the gate ahead of you.

CRYSTALS

NATURE'S ENERGY

Nature takes 10,000 years to create a piece of quartz crystal. Crystals are part of the 'aura' of Earth, energy in a crystallised form. Each crystal is unique and contains its own energy. Crystals are becoming increasingly popular as tools for meditation, psychic awareness and healing.

By meditating on crystal to enter a calm, receptive state and observing the thoughts, feelings and impressions you are receiving from your deep subconscious levels, you can develop your psychic awareness.

The crystal acts as a focus for concentration, to help the mind into a trance state whereupon visions appear. Some people leave crystals under their pillow, in order to 'replay' their dreams the following morning.

NUMEROLOGY

THE STUDY OF NUMBERS

Numerology – the study of numbers – is practised in many cultures around the world today and its roots can be traced back through many centuries.

It is based on a belief that numbers are not solid objects, but moving energies or vibrations. These vibrations influence our lives with either light or positive experiences (connection) or the dark shadow side or negative experiences (separation).

In numerology, numbers are not valued, as with money, but simply understood. Numerology can be used to determine the best time for major moves and activities in life, when to invest, when to marry, when to travel, when to change jobs or relocate.

There are various forms practised: Esoteric numerology explores concepts behind

numbers to reveal the inner mysteries of life and the universe; Chaldean numerology maintains that every digit has a unique vibration, the Kabbalah, or the application of the numerology within names, is also used; but Pythagorian Numerology remains one of the most popular methods of numerology practised in the West today.

NUMEROLOGY

THE STUDY OF NUMBERS

The basis of numerology is that who we are is influenced to some extent by our birth name and birth date, and both can be used to reveal two of the most significant numbers influencing your life – your Life Path Number and Personality Number.

Life Path Number

This is the sum of your birth date, it represents the native traits you will carry with you through life, and the nature of your life journey. Calculate your number by using the following formula (the digits of the month and year should treated as separate numbers and added together beforehand):
Day, 12 (12) + Month, November (1+1) + Year 1972 (1+9+7+2) = 33
3+3 = 6 = Life Path Number

Continue until the sum reaches a single digit (1-9), or the master numbers of 11 and 22.

1 You have the potential to be a good leader and your enthusiasm and determination, combined with originality, will help you reach your goals, however be careful of becoming selfish.

2 Diplomatic with a sensitive and fair approach to life. Harmony and routine are important to you but this can make you apathetic. Build upon your natural instincts of caring for others.

3 Bright, sociable and capable of excelling in some creative field. Your outgoing nature is complimented with a sensitive side, however, try not to lose sight of your purpose.

4 Trustworthy, practical, and a down-to-earth individual. Your organisational skills are exceptional. Your determination can be mistaken for stubbornness, but you deliver results. Be wary of becoming dogmatic.

NUMEROLOGY

THE STUDY OF NUMBERS

5 Seeking adventure, you value your freedom and independence. As a good communicator you should find challenges that involve others. Use your versatility, but don't become self indulgent.

6 A responsible, compassionate and generous personality, your home life is very important to you. Reliability, wisdom and understanding are some of your greatest talents. Be careful of interfering or becoming a slave to others.

7 Often reserved and analytical, you have great depth of thought. Although a loner you possess peace-loving and affectionate qualities. Maintain perspective to avoid developing negative attitudes.

8 Powerful, confident and materially successful, you are fiercely independent, and competitive. At your best you have the ability to achieve big things, however your conviction can border on dictatorial.

9 A caring, compassionate and generous person, your open heart and mind makes you a sociable person. However, it can be difficult for many to embrace the self-less nature of this path.

11 This master number is associated with spiritual awareness. Visionary and cultured, your ideas are often beyond the understanding of others. Maintain faith in your plans, you have the potential to produce something truly inspirational.

22 The second master number is the hardest to live up to. Idealistic but practical, you can envisage great things, but can also achieve them, limited only by your lack of effort. Succeeding should not be at the cost of others.

NUMEROLOGY

THE STUDY OF NUMBERS

Personality Number

This is taken from the full names by which you are usually known and shows your natural abilities and talents. To calculate your personality number, take each name separately and add up the letter values using the conversion chart below. Reduce each name to a single digit or master number. Then add the results of all of the names to arrive at a single or master number. You should only use your full name as it appears on your birth certificate, nicknames or married names should not be used, although in the case of adoption, your given adopted name should be used instead.

```
1 2 3 4 5 6 7 8 9
A B C D E F G H I
J K L M N O P Q R
S T U V W X Y Z
```

1 A natural leader, you are highly driven and often initiate action. Happiest working on your own, you make good use of your initiative and are a creative problem solver. However, do not dominate to succeed.

2 A team player you excel in the role of mediator. Although, modest, tactful and friendly you can be over-sensitive and shy.

3 With a creative talent, particularly with words, you are likely to thrive in the fields of writing, acting or sales. Although enthusiastic and highly sociable, you can slip into superficiality.

4 Good organisational skills, practicality and attention to detail means you are well suited to the technical. Loyal and sincere you take your responsibilities seriously. Your fastidious nature can develop into dogmatism.

5 A quick thinker, you are multi-talented and capable of turning your hand to most tasks. With good people skills you may

NUMEROLOGY

THE STUDY OF NUMBERS

enjoy the challenge of PR and sales work. Often restless, you should remember to think before taking action.

6 Responsible with a kind and generous spirit. You have a natural gift for working with the old, the young, the sick, or the underprivileged, but do not demand too much of yourself.

7 Logical and rational you seek out wisdom and truth (in either the scientific or spiritual realm). Open yourself to others and learn to trust people more.

8 Possessing good business sense and a practical side you are likely to succeed in the material sense. Mind that your ambition does not veer out of control.

9 Working well with people, you are sensitive to the needs of others and compassionate. Selfishness will breed if your natural characteristics to help others is ignored.

11 With an affinity with the arts you are intuitive and sensitive. Your idealistic plans can be inspired, but can lack practicality.

12 Extremely capable, you are able to turn almost any project into a success. Practical and perceptive, you possess powerful inner strength but this positive characteristic can become overbearing.

RAT	OX	TIGER	RABBIT	DRAGON	SNAKE	HORSE	GOAT	MONKEY	ROOSTER	DOG	PIG
1912	1913	1914	1915	1916	1917	1918	1919	1920	1921	1922	1923
1924	1925	1926	1927	1928	1929	1930	1931	1932	1933	1934	1935
1936	1937	1938	1939	1940	1941	1942	1943	1944	1945	1946	1947
1948	1949	1950	1951	1952	1953	1954	1955	1956	1957	1958	1959
1960	1961	1962	1963	1964	1965	1966	1967	1968	1969	1970	1971
1972	1973	1974	1975	1976	1977	1978	1979	1980	1981	1982	1983
1984	1985	1986	1987	1988	1989	1990	1991	1992	1993	1994	1995
1996	1997	1998	1999	2000	2001	2002	2003	2004	2005	2006	2007

CHINESE ASTROLOGY

AN ANCIENT ART

Chinese astrology has been practised for thousands of years, as a source of prediction and an indicator of personality. The Chinese use their religion and astrology to establish a harmony between people and the world around them.

Three systems are used for counting and classifying the years: The ten Heavenly Stems, the twelve Earthly Branches and the twelve Animals.

The twelve signs of the animals characterise the Chinese Lunar Calendar. The animal that rules your birth year has a deep influence on your life and learning the unique qualities of your sign can reveal your weaknesses and strengths. The twelve animals of Chinese astrology are considered to be a reflection of the universe itself. Chinese astrology can help you balance your yin and yang (yin is negative, dark and feminine; yang is positive, bright and masculine). You can also find out the type of person you are.

There are some legends about how the Chinese signs began, but no-one really knows. A popular one is that, once upon a time, the Lord Buddha summoned all the animals to come to him before he departed from Earth. Only twelve animals came to bid him farewell.

As a reward he named a year after each one in the order that they arrived. First came the Rat, then the Ox, the Tiger, Rabbit, Dragon, Snake, Horse, Sheep, Monkey, Rooster, Dog and Pig. Thus we have twelve signs today. To find out your own Chinese Sign, check the table of years. The Chinese calendar is based on the lunar year and starts in late January or early February. Study your sign carefully to use its features for your success. For years outside of the table just add or subtract, 60 years to find the correct sign.

CHINESE ASTROLOGY

AN ANCIENT ART

The Dragon is the most highly thought-of sign in the Chinese zodiac.

The Dog is known for its loyalty. They are very sincere.

The Rooster is highly observant and has good dress sense. They also like to be busy.

The Monkey is fun-loving, cheerful and always the centre of attention.

The Rabbit is shy and sensitive, and make a good friend.

The Pig is highly admired and make a good friend.

Chinese Astrology

AN ANCIENT ART

The Rat is quick witted and good at making money!

The Ox is strong willed and independent, but often stubborn.

The Snake is intelligent and charming, but watch out – they are good at telling lies!

The Horse is headstrong and independent, but very fun loving.

The Tiger is brave, proud, and make very good leaders.

The Goat is gentle, artistic and fond of nature.

ASTROLOGY

SIGNS OF THE ZODIAC

Astrology is the belief that the positions of the planets at the moment of a person's birth have a direct influence on their personality and the way they lead their lives.

Astrology is an extremely ancient art. Around 4,000 BC, the Sumerian people first worshiped the Sun, Moon and Venus. It was practised in the temples, where it was blended with religious elements.

Around the third millennium BC, astrology was being used by rulers to predict the fate of nations: war or peace, famine or plenty. The Chinese were also skilled astronomers, and some experts believe that Chinese astronomy may extend as far back as 5,000 BC.

The zodiac consists of twelve signs. These are divided into four elements – earth, fire, water and air – all of which influence the character of each sign.

ASTROLOGY

SIGNS OF THE ZODIAC

Aries 21 March – 20 April, Fire Sign

Aries is the leader, the symbol of individuality. Arian virtues are honesty and enthusiasm although they can sometimes be accused of arrogance and intolerance.

Taurus 21 April – 21 May, Earth Sign

Taurus is the sign of loyalty. Taureans have great determination and faithfulness, but can be obstinate and unwilling to take risks.

Gemini 22 May – 20 June, Air Sign

Gemini is the sign of the twins. It represents duality in all areas, good and evil, conscious and unconscious. for example. Gemini are skilled in resolving contradiction, but are frequently unable to put their ideas into action.

Astrology

SIGNS OF THE ZODIAC

Cancer 22 June – 23 July, Water Sign

Cancer is the sign of excessive emotion. Cancerians need to learn to think clearly, however, when they are emotionally committed to their goals, they give their all to achieving success.

Leo 24 July – 23 August, Fire Sign

Leo is the sign of the Sun, and like the Sun, Leos are always at the centre of things. They have to remember to give other people a chance to shine, though.

Virgo 24 August – 22 September, Earth Sign

Virgo is the sign of dedication and hard work. Virgoans are selfless and serve others well, but they do have a tendency to judge themselves and others far too harshly.

ASTROLOGY

SIGNS OF THE ZODIAC

Libra 23 September — 23 October, Air Sign

Libra is the sign of harmony and balance. Librans' strengths are their firm belief in fairness and justice. Their weakness is their inability to make up their mind.

Scorpio 24 October — 22 November, Water Sign

Scorpio is a mysterious sign, renowned for its passion. It represents regeneration and loyalty to friends. Their weaknesses are a readiness to bear a grudge and seek revenge.

Sagittarius 23 November — 20 December, Fire Sign

Sagittarius is the sign of the adventurer. Sagittarians' strengths are their energy and enthusiasm. Their weakness tends to be their lack of consistency.

ASTROLOGY

SIGNS OF THE ZODIAC

CAPRICORN *21 December — 20 January, Earth Sign*

Those born under the sign of Capricorn are hard workers. Capricorns are devoted to duty, but unwilling to take risks.

AQUARIUS *21 January — 19 February, Air Sign*

Aquarius is the sign of the revolutionary. Their strengths are inventive genius and strongly-held ideas. Aquarians' weakness is a lack of co-operation.

PISCES *20 February — 20 March, Water Sign*

Pisces is the wisest of the signs. Pisceans are selfless and idealistic. Their weaknesses are confusion and escapism.

DREAMS

INTERPRETING AND UNDERSTANDING

Long before the studies of Swiss psychologist Carl Jung, dreams were considered to be signs of the future.

The Native Americans interpreted their dreams as signs of inner well-being. The Inuit people of North America considered dreams to be an important source of information about future events and making decisions. The Inuit believe that animal spirits use the language of dreams to communicate with humans.

If you consider that there may be many levels of existence happening at the same time, it's very conceivable that dreams could pick up material from other time frames or parallel realities that we aren't aware of in our conscious world.

Dreamcatchers, (circular in appearance, with a webbed centre and, often decorated with beads and feathers,) are believed to be able to 'trap' dreams. To Native Americans, dreamcatchers were symbolic nets used to harness the positive energies of dreams and act as talismans. Feathers bound in red thread were hung over a sleeping area or attached to dreamcatchers, which caught positive dreams and retained their influence in the dreamer's waking life.

READING TEA LEAVES

TASSEOGRAPHY

Tasseography, sometimes called tasseomancy, is the practice of divination through the interpretation of the tea leaf patterns left in the bottom of a cup after a person has finished drinking.

This art actually originated in China around 2,000 years ago, but it has also been associated with Eastern European Gypsies, the Scots, and the Irish, among others.

It became popular in Europe, during the eighteenth century when tea first became popular, and is still of importance today, although tea drinkers nowadays are more partial to tea bags, which obviously can't be read.

To read someone's tea leaves, you first need to set up the cup for a reading. It is best to use tea brewed without a strainer so that you have enough tea leaves. Make sure your subject leaves enough tea in the cup to enable you to move the leaves around easily. Ask them to slowly move the remaining tea in the cup around three times clockwise slowly in the cup by holding the handle at an angle. Then invite them to turn the cup over onto a saucer.

READING TEA LEAVES

TASSEOGRAPHY

The next step is trying to comprehend the individual symbols, so you can determine their significance. When doing this, it's best just to use your intuition to tell you what the symbols mean. Don't worry about misinterpreting the image.

Trust your first reaction to the tea leaves and their position, if you thought it looked vaguely like a bear when you first glanced into the cup — then that is what it is.

The final part is interpreting the meaning. Since the handle represents the subject of the reading, the things closest to the handle are the things which are closest to the subject and have the most influence. The things on the opposite side of the cup have the least influence. Also, everything on the rim of the cup is the near future and everything at the very bottom of the cup is very far in the future, with logical progression in between.

Numbers which you see in the leaves are usually indications of time. If it is in the bottom of the cup, you can think of it in years, and if it is nearer the rim, in hours or days. Letters are usually the initials of people who will be of influence to the person whose tea leaves are being read.

READING TEA LEAVES

TASSEOGRAPHY

A brief guide to the symbols in your cup:

Anchor a problem will be answered
Apple good health and happiness
Arrow (down) bad luck
Arrow (up) good luck
Axe you will be rid of burdens
Bird good luck will arrive
Bone be cautious
Bridge a time for change and travel
Castle expect a legacy
Chicken change is on the way
Clouds worry
Eagle courage
Egg success is likely
Face change is likely
Fire foolishness will destroy something
Hat visitor
Heart love
Key secrets

Lake peace
Loop avoid acting on impulse
Monkey stop, think
Palm Tree creativity
Seahorse self-indulgence is necessary
Shark trouble
Swarm of bees a gathering is close
Sword move quickly
Tower events will take an unexpected turn
Triangle child
Vase a friend is in need of advice or consolation
Volcano things are about to come to a head
Web an omen
Wheel a sign of progress
Windmill a personal venture will succeed
Wings an interesting message is on its way
Yacht money worries will lessen

DICE PREDICTION

ANCIENT FORTUNE-TELLING

Dice have been used for centuries to indicate fate and they are possibly one of the most ancient of all systems of divination.

Dice are intended to be used purely for fortune-telling rather than to give an insight into a situation. To try dice divination, take three dice and mark out a large circle on the floor or on a board. Cup the three dice in your hand and focus your attention on the dice. Lightly shake the dice and throw them into the circle. Ignore any dice that fall outside the circle.

If they all fall outside the circle, no fortune can be read on that day. Add up the numbers on the top face of dice inside the circle and consult the list on the opposite page for the meaning.

DICE PREDICTION

ANCIENT FORTUNE-TELLING

1. A new arrival, a baby, or an unexpected sum of money.
2. A road that forks two ways, but the longest road is best.
3. A pleasant surprise and the granting of wishes.
4. A disappointment.
5. A stranger coming soon, will bring with them happiness.
6. There may be a material loss, but an increase in spiritual or emotional wealth.
7. Gossip and spite should be ignored.
8. An unwise course that will lead to blame.
9. Joy in love – maybe even a wedding.
10. Family happiness, leading to a meeting that will bring new opportunities in the business world.
11. Illness or unhappiness in someone close will be resolved.
12. A letter needing a quick decision – seek sound advice.
13. Tears and sorrow.
14. A new admirer who will soon become close.
15. The need to avoid being drawn into intrigue or trouble by others.
16. A pleasant and profitable journey, but delays must be avoided.
17. Journeys overseas, or dealings with those from overseas, will be advantageous.
18. A great profit or promotion within a short period.

DOWSING & DIVINING

MAGNETIC EARTH

As well as searching for underground water, minerals or other objects, queries into the future (in the form of answers to yes-or-no questions) can be found using a divining device.

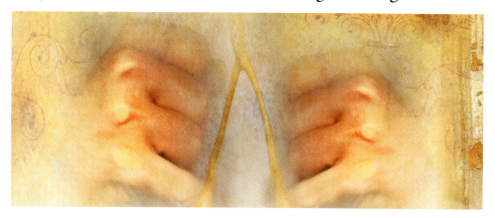

Traditionally, a forked rod of hazel or apple wood was used, but a pair of L-shaped metal rods or a pendulum are also typically used.

Dowsing is an ancient activity. Cave paintings estimated to be at least 8,000 years old, depicting a group of people watching someone who appears to be dowsing with a forked stick, have been discovered in the Tassili-n-Ajjer mountains in the Sahara Desert.

DOWSING & DIVINING

MAGNETIC EARTH

The Old Testament of the Bible also contains reference to dowsing — Moses used a divining rod to find water in the desert when leading his people to the Promised Land.

When wood is used, the twig points downwards without conscious effort by the dowser, when water is reached. One explanation is that the twig is pulled down by the water's magnetic energy field. When metal rods are used, held pointing forwards and parallel, they swing inwards or outwards over the search object. These work in the same way when a question about the future is asked.

PENDULUM POWER

BOY OR GIRL?

The pendulum is used widely by professional dowsers or water diviners, who often prefer it to the divining rod. A pendulum is a weight made of wood, metal, glass or crystal, suspended on the end of a cord.

Pendulums are often used for divinatory purposes. A person will ask a question, to which the answer must be yes or no. When it swings, the dowser interprets its prediction, for example, clockwise rotation may mean yes, anti-clockwise, no.

Pendulums are popular for determining issues such as personal health. Locating the source of disease or negative energy in the body, or even to determine the gender of an unborn baby, for example.

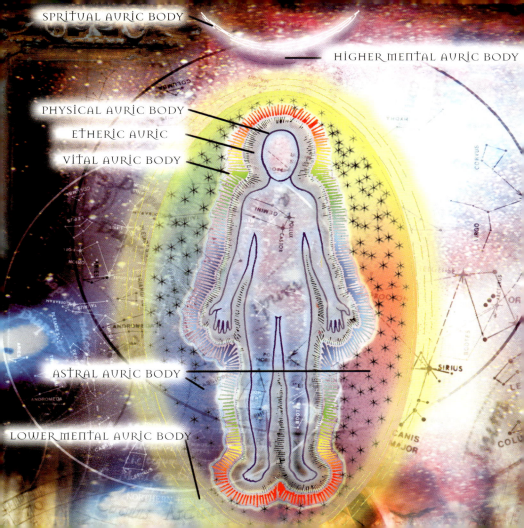

AURA READING

BODY ENERGY

Auras are energy bodies that emanate from any physical being, with electro-magnetic energy containing information about your deepest self.

Aura's reflect our mental activity and emotional state. Although invisible to the naked eye, psychics can read a person's aura to ascertain their health, emotions and future guidance. Auras come in many shapes, sizes, colours and textures.

Human auras radiate complex patterns and forms of light. Religious books sometimes refer to light as an attribute of mankind and say that this is our true nature. In early Christian and Buddhist paintings, the aura has often been depicted as an area of light radiating from the body or the head.

Anyone has the potential to see an aura. Just relax your body and mind, choose an object or person to look at, and gaze slightly behind them. When you are calm, aura vision will come to you. Auras are made up of seven main elements, which are all interconnected.

AURA READING

BODY ENERGY

The Physical Auric Body

This layer, begins at the edge of the skin and extends out about 4 cm. It is usually a shade of blue, and relates to the condition and health of the physical body.

The Etheric Auric Body

Extending from the Physical Auric Body about 2–10 cm in all directions from the body. To the novice, it appears as a dense layer of pale smoke. The practised viewer will see different colours.

The Vital Auric Body

This aura layer begins at the outer edge of the Etheric Auric Body, and extends out about 5–15 cm, sometimes up to 30 cm. It appears as rainbow-coloured fingers of light. This body is the auric layer in which our emotions operate.

The Astral Auric Body

This can be anything from 10 cm to several metres wide, extending from the outer edge of the Vital Auric Body. Within this aura are our thoughts and mental processes. Thoughts take on different forms, from tear drops, which grow in the aura as ideas become concrete, to spirals and stars, which accompany prayer and inspiration.

The Lower Mental Auric Body

Usually 4–17 cm. wide, this layer is a bright yellow colour. It displays a person's abilities on the intellectual level.

The Higher Mental Auric Body

Usually violet to dark blue, when spirit communication is taking place, the entity stimulates the higher mental layer of the aura, causing it to radiate in various shades.

The Spiritual Auric Body

This has been described as a radiant white light. It is pure energy. This layer is referred to as the link to God.

AURA READING

BODY ENERGY

Chakras are energy whirlpools where incoming energy is processed and channelled around the body and outgoing energy is expelled.

They form a line from the top of the head along the spine and down to the tailbone. There are seven major centres and several minor chakras points around the body.

The first of these is located at the base of the spine, disruptions in the auric layer surrounding this area can be related to the individual suffering from immune system related diseases or deep insecurities.

The second major chakra is located above the genitals and below the naval. Agitation in this area show emotional problems. Serious emotional problems outwardly manifest themselves as physical problems in the stomach, ovaries, testicles, pancreas and the colon.

The third chakra is found in the solar plexus and this energy is all about personal power and creativity. People with disruptions in this area show outward symptoms of timidness and fear.

The fourth chakra, is in the chest, level with the heart muscle, and relates to passion and love. When it is damaged the individual can have difficulties showing compassion and giving, or receiving, affection.

The fifth chakra located in the throat relates to communication within ourselves and with others. Disturbances to this chakra bring up discipline issues and an inability to express one's self.

The sixth chakra is in the centre of the brain and is where your spiritual sight functions. Imbalance in this area creates outward suffering, such as sleep disorders, hallucinations and hormonal problems.

The seventh major chakra is of the highest spiritual order and is all about our true self. Any disorder in this area needs serious attention as a blockage in this area can stop the flow of vital cosmic energy which is needed to evolve.

CONCLUSION

THE FUTURE

Attempting to foretell the future has been around for generations, and will probably continue for many years to come. Hopefully after reading this book, you will have a clearer understanding of a large selection of the most common forms of prediction.

Some of the prediction methods not covered here are stichomancy, Bibliomancy, angel cards, medicine cards, biorhythms, tattwa cards, and forms of divination by a number of objects, such as ghosts, meteors, birds, snakes, arrows, dots made at random on paper, laughter, and even the colour and peculiarities of wine!

Some people do not attempt to guess the future, preferring instead to wait to see which hand life will deal them. So, is it truly possible to be able to read the future? There's only one way to find out...